The Wonder Dish

for Margie Knight

Praise for John Mole:

'A new John Mole collection is good news.'
Anne Harvey, The Guardian

'Never a phrase too many, never one short, always
demonstrating that there is infinitely more to a good
poem than the number of words on the page.
The work of a true poet.'
Charles Causley

Other collections by John Mole for children:

Boo to a Goose
The Mad Parrot's Countdown
Catching the Spider
The Conjuror's Rabbit
Hot Air
The Dummy's Dilemma

The Wonder Dish

Poems by John Mole

Illustrated by Bee Willey

OXFORD
UNIVERSITY PRESS

OXFORD
UNIVERSITY PRESS

Great Clarendon Street, Oxford OX2 6DP

Oxford University Press is a department of the University of Oxford.
It furthers the University's objective of excellence in research, scholarship,
and education by publishing worldwide in

Oxford New York

Athens Auckland Bangkok Buenos Aires
Cape Town Chennai Dar es Salaam Delhi Hong Kong Istanbul
Karachi Kolkata Kuala Lumpur Madrid Melbourne Mexico City Mumbai
Nairobi São Paulo Shanghai Taipei Tokyo Toronto

Oxford is a registered trade mark of Oxford University Press
in the UK and in certain other countries

British Library Cataloguing in Publication Data available

ISBN 0-19-276308-3

1 3 5 7 9 10 8 6 4 2

Typeset by Mary Tudge (Typesetting Services)
Designed by Jo Samways
Printed at Cox & Wyman Ltd, Reading, Berks

Contents

Yummy
ideas and
words an
sentences of colour
and sounds and t
shapes and letters

First Impressions

Put them down quickly however they come
in whatever order, let them go where they will
like laying the table in a rush.
This is a meal for one though we're all hungry.
Where are your manners? Forget them.
Think about holding back a little later
when you're making the arrangements
and the spread is there. Perhaps then
the refinement of a paper napkin
or a place-name for your teacher, but for now
the improvised solo banquet, the acceptable
measure of your greed, wolfing each
syllable as a taster, licking your fingers
as the words arrive. Go on, indulge yourself
before you send the invitations,
grab and mix for the sheer confectionary
thrill of it, the savoury, the sweet,
the raw, the cooked, the wonder-dish
served up by language for a gathering
you'll soon become the host of. Put them
all down, all the sounds, the colours,
as they come, a bumper feast in readiness
and only one word for the sum of it: enjoy.

Pocket the Stone

Pocket the stone
your mother made soup from,
press the last leaf
of the family tree,
pinch thin air
between your fingers,
pass into life
unharmed and free.

Sharpen the blade
your father fashioned,
sound the first note
on the messenger's horn,
sift fine gold
through a broken hour-glass,
search for the rose
which has no thorn.

Once in a Dream

Once in a dream
I gazed at the mirror
and all I could see
was tomorrow forever.

Once in a dream
I started counting
One, two, three
and I couldn't stop.

Once in a dream
the clock ticked backwards
and I watched its hands
going faster and faster.

Once in a dream
snow began falling
and ice grew thick
in the middle of summer.

Once in a dream
I walked through a forest
ignoring the voices
which cried *Go Home!*

Once in a dream
I conquered a mountain
and planted my flag
to say I'd arrived.

Once in a dream
I felt so happy
that I danced through the night
to invisible music.

Once in a dream
I missed a heart-beat
but you were beside me
and took my hand.

The Doctor and the Clown

A sad man went to the doctor
Who took one look and guessed
That his visitor wasn't physically ill
But was certainly depressed.

'You're right, so right,' said the sad man,
'And I doubt if there's any cure
But I thought I should come to see you
Just to make doubly sure.'

'I'm glad that you did,' said the doctor
With a great big smile on his face,
'Because, as it just so happens,
You've come to the right place.

I'm not going to give you a tonic,
I'm not going to give you a pill,
But I am going to give you a word of advice
And take it if you will.

Last night I went to the circus
Which has just arrived in town
With a whole array of wonderful acts
But the best of them all is the clown.

Grock is his name, and believe me
He's really a clown and a half,
He'll double you up in stitches
And remind you how to laugh.

I can guarantee when you see him
Your troubles will melt away,
So book yourself a ringside seat
At once, without delay.'

The sad man thanked him, turned to go
And shuffled towards the door
While the doctor noticed that he looked
Even sadder than before.

'Take my word for it,' said the doctor,
'At least give the clown a chance.'
The sad man summoned a rueful smile
And looked at him askance.

Then it suddenly occurred to the doctor
To ask the patient's name,
'I know all about your problem
And the reason why you came

But who exactly are you?'
The sad man bowed his head.
'Haven't you guessed already?
I *am* Grock,' he said.

The Philosopher's Puzzle

When I did my sums next door
I knew that two and two made four
But now that I'm here I'm not so sure.

So I add them up once more
And get the same answer as before
But what have they become next door?

Now that I'm here I'm not so sure
That I am who I was before
When I was there. My brain feels sore

Which wasn't how it was next door
Where I knew that two and two made four
And not one less and not one more

But maybe none of us can be sure
Here, there, or anywhere any more
That two and two are always four

So in this world of either/or
If what seems wrong seemed right before
Let's hope it will all add up next door.

Cuckoo Jones

When he thought he heard
The first cuckoo of spring,
Said Mr Jones
'Now there's a thing!'

So he picked up his pen
And wrote to *The Times*,
Just a small letter,
Just a few lines.

But they printed it
As they used to do—
The first *Times* reader
To hear the cuckoo.

That was years ago.
Now he walks down our street
With a shrunken body
And shuffling feet.

Through the skin of his face
You can see the bones,
But we all still love
Mr Cuckoo Jones.

Biggles' Last Testament

I, Major James (Biggles) Bigglesworth,
being of sound mind
but beginning to be bored out of it,
am leaving this will behind.

I scorn the post-prandial haven
of an elderly club armchair.
Chaps should meet their maker
face-to-face in mid-air.

Then whether they escape the flak
or spiral into a dive,
they'll have kept the bulldog spirit
gloriously alive.

So time for one final take-off
as I stiffen my upper lip
and reassure poor Ginger
that it's *just another trip!*

Can't take you with me, laddie,
I'm going solo, old scout.
No one argues with Biggles.
Over and out.

But I've left him a fleece-lined jacket,
its pockets stuffed with maps,
and made sure he's got money enough
to buy drinks for the other chaps.

And I've left him my second-best goggles,
(I'll be wearing my favourite ones)
as well as a set of phrase-books
for coping with 'foreign tongues'.

So it's up and away and God save the King
but I tell you, before I go,
that death is a great adventure
and that life's been a jolly good show.

Superheroes

I'm sick of Superheroes!
I think they're over-rated.
They're just dull blokes
With flashy cloaks
Whose egos are inflated.

I'm sick of Superheroes!
With all the girls they meet
Instead of flowers
It's special powers
That knock them off their feet.

I'm sick of Superheroes!
I hate their perfect teeth,
Their laser stare,
Their sculpted hair
With no brains underneath.

I'm sick of Superheroes!
They're utterly unreal.
They never cry,
Don't seem to die,
And call a car 'mobile'.

So down with Superheroes!
Although I must admit
That in a way . . .
Well, I have to say
I envy them a bit.

The Sad Story of Terrible Trevor

Terrible Trevor Alucard
Reckoned himself, he said, 'Well hard'.
His favourite time was after dark.
He stalked the streets, he prowled the park.
'Where are you going?' his mum would shout
And Trev would always answer 'Out!'
At first, it seemed to him enough
To do the usual scary stuff,
Just walk about in studs and leather,
Chains and buckles and whatever
But soon he found this rather boring
Like playing football without scoring.

'What can I do tomorrow night
To give everyone a proper fright?'
He asked himself, then scratched his head.
'The trouble with this town—it's dead!'
To tell the truth you'd seldom find
A fresh thought crossing Trevor's mind,
But suddenly he cried out 'Hey,
The churchyard's got a right of way
Past all those crosses, angels' wings,
And stones and spooky graves and things.
It's just the place to hang around,
To tiptoe up without a sound
And then with a blood-curdling cry
To leap out on any passers-by.'

So next day he spent his pocket-money
(All of it, every single penny)
On a cloak and fangs—vampire attire—
From *Van Helsing's Costume Hire*
And took it home. 'What's that you've got?'
Asked Trevor's mum. 'I'll tell you what,
Mind your own business, woman!' Sad,
But Trev gave answers like his dad
And just like Dad he snarled and swore
Then stomped upstairs and slammed the door.

So night arrived and, fit to burst,
Trev was ready to do his worst.
I tell you, he could hardly wait
To dress up at the churchyard gate.
Once there he donned his vampire kit,
Just as he'd hoped, a perfect fit.
Now for a passer-by to scare.
As if the answer to a prayer
And much to Trevor's cruel delight
A hurrying figure came in sight.
At first it seemed to be the vicar
Except he was moving rather quicker,

Sort of floating down the path
With a sort of rather nasty laugh
(Crepuscular and melancholy)
Which Trev could tell was far from holy,
And then, alas,—Oh send us grace!—
The two of them met face to face
Like shadows looking in a mirror,
One with a grin, the other terror.
This was now way beyond a joke.
The grin flashed pointed fangs then spoke:

'My, what a silly boy you are,
Pretending to be Dracula
When anyone can see that you
Really haven't got a clue
About blood suction and all that.
You couldn't scare a witch's cat!
Your cloak's too short, your fangs are fake,
Your whole equipment's a mistake,
You should be drinking Seven-Up
Or bedtime cocoa from a cup
Instead of scaring little kids
With talk of garlic, coffin lids,
And all the necks you're going to bite.
Still, Trev, since we've met tonight
We might as well become acquainted
(By this time Trev had nearly fainted!)
So shut your eyes and count to ten.
You won't have to pretend again.
Our meeting here is most fortuitous.
I need an apprentice, Trev, and you it is!
You've an awful lot to learn, I know,
But you're keen enough, it seems. Let's go,
Tomorrow is another day
And Transylvania's quite a way!'

With that, a flash and a clap of thunder
A cloak was swirled and Trev tucked under.
He might have given a muffled shout
But there was nobody else about
Except the cold dead, long engraved,
Indifferent to how a boy behaved
And, anyway, far too deep to hear
Or, if they did, too late to care.
Now, in the churchyard, one more stone
Under the yew tree all alone
Says Trevor Alucard RIP
Except he *doesn't*, believe you me!

I Spy

My black gloves are shiny,
My glasses are dark,
I wait on a bench
By a lake in the park.

My face is a blank
As the world passes by
Which is one of the things
About being a spy.

What I've learned to be good at
Is just sitting tight
With occasional glances
To left and to right

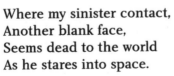

Then getting up slowly
And creeping along
At a pre-arranged time
To the next bench on

Where my sinister contact,
Another blank face,
Seems dead to the world
As he stares into space.

His black gloves are shiny,
His glasses are dark,
So we sit side by side
By a lake in the park.

What's New?

Haven't you grown
says my gran
since I last saw you.
Oh, my very own
not so little man,
how I adore you!

She doesn't half
go on. Every time
it's the same old spiel
and they all laugh
politely, and I'm
supposed to as well.

I mean, I don't ever
tell her *Granny, oh,*
you've started to shrink!
No, I'd never never
dream of it, no,
but that's what I think.

Perhaps when she's
much much older
(when I am too)
then just for a tease
I'll tap her on the shoulder
and ask *What's new?*

But is there new in it?

A looking-glass with you in it,
A sticky tube with glue in it,
A map with Timbuctoo in it,
An old box with a shoe in it,
A space-ship with a crew in it,
An owl with a tu-whoo in it,
A cage with a cockatoo in it,
A cry with boo hoo hoo in it,
A kitten with a mew in it,
A paintbox with royal blue in it,
A sneeze with a *kerchoo!* in it,
A bathroom with shampoo in it,
A school hall with a queue in it,
A churchyard with a yew in it,
A band with a kazoo in it,
A poem with much ado in it . . .
Rhymes? There are quite a few in it,
And this last line has got NEW in it!

What It Was Like

The day my bike brakes failed
on a steep hill near home
I squeezed and squeezed them
tight up to the handle-bars
and nothing happened
as I sped against the wind
with terrified eyes clamped shut.

It was like when I had this dream
of switching off my radio
and when I felt the click
a voice I recognized
but couldn't put a name or face to
just went on and on and on
as if it knew I wasn't going to wake.

What the Neighbours Say

Look at that car going
Down our street
With those two kids arguing
In the back seat.

It's the Jackson family
Off to France.
Will they get there easily?
No chance.

'Thump, ouch, pinch, grr,
Leave me alone!'
Then, oh, *mon dieu*,
Comes the journey home.

Bouncer

Bouncer bounces like nobody's business,
the promise of will-be, the essence of is-ness,
the magic of growing, the full-steam-ahead,
the fizz in the cola, the yeast in the bread,
while his parents and teachers for all they are worth
try to bring him a little more down to earth.

Experts on Bounce never tire of pronouncing
on the how and the why and the wherefore of bouncing
but whether it's measured by grams or the ounce
a bounce is a bounce is a bounce is a bounce
so Bouncer keeps bouncing at home and at school
like nobody's business, like nobody's fool.

The Animal Alphabet

A is for ant-eater with its long snout,
B is for bats which zig-zag about,
C for the chimp who swings from a branch,
D for the donkey asleep after lunch,
E is for elephant, wrinkly and grey,
F for the fox which I hope gets away,
G for giraffe with its JCB neck,
H is the hen with a husband to peck,
I for an indolent iguana,
J for the shape of the monkey's banana,
K for koala who clings to a tree,
L for the leopard whose spots won't change me,
M is for Mole, my namesake, of course,
N for the neigh of a bad-tempered horse,
O is the ostrich whose head disappears
And (wait for it, wait for it, cover your ears)
P for the parrot which squawks till you're deaf,
Q is for quails' eggs, a treat from the chef,
R for rhinoceros, beware its huge horn,
S for the sloth who's too lazy to yawn,
T is the tiger, that striped mega-star,
U is for ugly which no creatures are,
V is for vole, so nearly my name
(Just change the first letter and read it again),
W watch out for Ahab's white whale,
X for the slobbery kiss of a snail,
Y for the Yogi in Yellowstone Park,
Zzzz for the forest asleep after dark.

Potatoes

One potato two potato
three potato four

sniff them feel them
scrub them peel them
and bounce them on the floor

five potato six potato
seven potato eight

slice them boil them
fry them in oil then
shovel them onto your plate

nine potato ten potato
eleven potato twelve

gobble them swallow them
pudding to follow them
making a pig of yourself

twelve potato eleven potato
ten potato nine

I'll swap you that one
a tit for your tat one
but this potato's mine

eight potato seven potato
six potato five

there's a worm in my gravy
all wriggly and wavy
I think he's still alive

four potato three potato
two potato one

what a horrible dinner
it wasn't a winner
thank goodness it's over and done

Frozen Doughnuts

Homer, Maggie,
Bart and Lisa
Left their doughnuts
In the freezer.

Lisa, Homer,
Bart and Maggie
Found them
In a paper baggie.

Maggie, Lisa,
Homer, Bart,
Waiting for
TV to start.

Bart and Maggie,
Lisa, Homer,
All together
On the sofa.

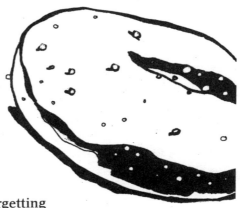

Not forgetting
Mother Marge,
She's the grown-up,
She's in charge.

Silly Simpsons
Watching telly,
Eat my shorts
And slap my belly.

Itchy, Scratchy,
Crusty too
But frozen doughnuts
Just won't do.

My Family and Other Animals

I saw an elephant skip down the street
I saw my sister trying to count her feet
I saw a lady centipede in striped pyjamas
I saw my brother bound for the Bahamas
I saw a Jumbo Jet try on new shoes
I saw my mum eat chocolate puppy chews
I saw a full-grown dog shampoo the car
I saw my dad swing on an iron bar
I saw a monkey reading Harry Potter
I saw my best friend look like a whiskery otter
I saw a wet cat in a rocking chair
I saw my granny coming up for air
I saw a dolphin falling fast asleep
I saw my grandpa on the rubbish heap
I saw a chicken's wish-bone good as new
I saw my old bike feeding at the zoo

Abner's Leap
(for Peter Scupham & Margaret Steward)

At Old Hall, on the Norwich Road,
A certain cat makes his abode,
A cat not overweight but stout,
A cat who likes to leap about
And land his bulk judiciously
Wherever it seems good to be,
Wherever life allows a space
For musing on the human race
Or gently purring off to sleep
To dream of yet another leap,
That grand, subversive frisky one,
That downright, final, risky one
With no cat's-cradle safety net,
To be no more the household pet
But dangerously debonair
And ready to land anywhere.
Abner, may you wake one day
To chance that leap, then we shall say
Oh, best of cats, Lord of Old Hall,
You're an example to us all.

Strange Meeting
(an old rhyme re-written)

Yesterday, a curious pair,
We met each other on the stair,
Me and that man who wasn't there.

Perhaps we'll meet again today,
But this time I intend to say
(That's if he hasn't gone away)
'So there you are, and here I stay!'

Ghosts and Gardens

Step by step the sun goes down
and its last rite
is a laying out of shadows.

*

Beside a gate, a stile.
Crossing from here to there
the ghosts go single file,
climb down and disappear.

*

Head cocked, half-
way down the trunk
a squirrel stops and listens.

*

Arms reach out
for the ghost of a tree house
suddenly abandoned
and the plaited rope
its children climbed.

*

Up at the Great Hall
when anyone walks though a wall
nobody bothers at all.

The Unsuccessful Conjuror

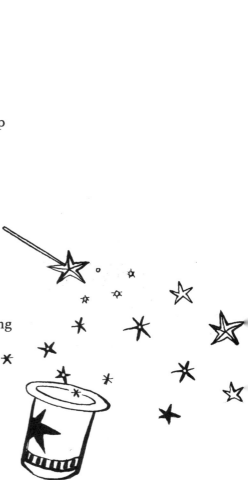

Whenever I'm stuck
and my tricks go wrong
someone in the audience
starts this song:

abracadabra,
just like that,
you've got no rabbit
and you've lost your hat.

When my face cracks up
with its silly grin,
they know the words
so they all join in:

abracadabra,
just like that,
you've got no rabbit
and you've lost your hat.

When the curtain falls
at the end of the show
I can hear them shouting
as I pack up to go:

abracadabra,
just like that,
you've got no rabbit
and you've lost your hat.

As I sneak off home
this familiar refrain
echoes in my head
again and again:

abracadabra,
just like that,
you've got no rabbit
and you've lost your hat.

As I walk through the door,
time after time
my wife and kids
greet me with this rhyme:

abracadabra,
just like that,
you've got no rabbit
and you've lost your hat.

And when I get to heaven
as I hope to do
most probably the angels
will sing along too:

abracadabra,
just like that,
you've got no rabbit
and you've lost your hat.

But when I reach
the celestial throne
perhaps God will show me
a trick of his own,

how, abracadabra,
just like that,
he produced the whole world
out of his hat!

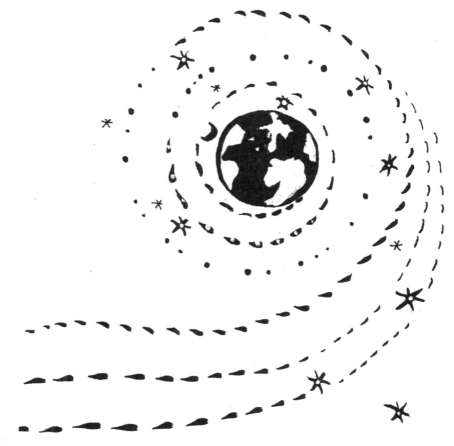

At the Pantomime

Yes, it was great to laugh
When one of the ugly sisters thought she was more beautiful
Than her other half,
And it was fun to cheer
When out of the magic lantern with a puff of smoke
We saw the genie appear,
And it was time to weep
When Snow White bit into the shiny apple
Or Beauty pricked her finger and fell asleep,
And it was really good
When the Prince arrived to wake them up
Though of course we knew that he would,
But best of all
When the villain sneaked on
(And, no, we didn't really want him to be gone)
It was absolute bliss
To hiss!

The Lights

This, then, is how Dad
did the lights. He had
to find them first,
remember where he'd put them.

Always the same place year
by year, and each year
he'd forgotten. *Try
the loft, Dad*. Bingo!

In a shoe-box, tangled
with the decorations—
brittle globes (always at least
one smashed), a raffia angel

and a sheriff's star. I'd
watch him separate the flex,
plug in, then
sure as Christmas was tomorrow

nothing happened. What
he didn't cry was
Bingo! Something far
less Christmassy, a word

which if I'd used it
I'd have gone straight
to my room for. Only after
muttering at fuses, twisting

spares in petalled
plastic sockets, switching
on and off and on
commanding me to cross

my fingers, came
a magic twinkling blaze
along the floor. We lifted it,
just Dad and me,

and oh so carefully
we wound that lit flex
round and in and out
of prickly branches

as a few dry needles
crackled on the presents
underneath. At last
the tree was ready

and we called the others in
to see the job we'd done,
as I do now each
Christmas with my son.

The Christmas Tree

Light up, Christmas tree! we children cried
at our village carol service, a falsetto
shriek to lift the roof. He couldn't hide
his smile, then let us have another go
when nothing happened. Evidently this
was God and plain old-fashioned manners
meeting for a trick too good to miss,
a grey-haired mischief-loving vicar's
showmanship while a unison of puzzled faces
gazed at the festooned, unlit marvel
wondering what went wrong. *Ah, yes,*
we forgot the magic word! All shall be well,
of course, when children are polite. *Say 'Please'*
together now, then go down on your knees.

Poor Poet

Once he used to sit there chewing his pencil,
Writing a few words, rubbing them out,
Tearing up sheet after sheet of paper,
Leaving his desk, wandering about

Then back again to the same procedure,
Scratching his head, rumpling his hair,
With not much to show for the hours spent
Chewing his pencil and sitting there.

Now, though, he gazes at a screen,
Still with little or nothing to say,
But somehow finding it so much easier
To switch off and walk away.

Answer Phone

Please leave your name.
I shall call you back.
There is no one here.
Do you have a number?

Do you have a cat?
I have four children.
They keep me busy.
They should be back.

I shall call your number.
My mind is empty.
There is no one there.
Please leave my name.

Please leave my cat.
He has no number.
Do you want four children?
They have names.

Please name your children.
My cat is Rover.
He will call you back.
I keep him busy.

Absolutely
(circa 1950)

Listen to me, yes
you, the pair of you
wasting your time
like this, and it's absolutely
no use giving me
a look like that
because you promised you'd be back
three hours ago, John
where's your cap? and Janet
haven't I told you
never . . . ? Don't you dare
go telling me
that Dan's the man, I'll
Mekon you the Mekon!
and another thing
yes, John, it's absolutely
no use thinking Dad'll buy you
that Converter set
unless you buckle down
and as for you
young lady I'd have thought
by now you'd learnt
your lesson, don't imagine
that I can't guess
just where you get your
ideas from . . . I mean I wonder
absolutely sometimes
why I even bother . . .
what's the use?

Old Wilkinson

Old Wilkinson's car was a clapped-out banger.
He clattered to school in it. Phut. Phut. Phut.
His face, on arrival, was bright red for danger.
'Don't begin sentences with *and* or *but!*'

A piece of snapped chalk was his lethal weapon.
It bounced from your head with a ricochet
And shot off at your neighbour, oh, cruel precision,
'No, I'm not in a very good mood today!'

It was anyone's guess who would be his next victim.
Lessons with him were like Russian roulette.
Your tight-fitting desk was the prison you sat in—
'Dim-wits like you deserve all that you get!'

Then, straight after class, he'd rush off to the car-park
To rev up his engine with a cloud of exhaust
Having left us a heap of impossible homework
For brains overloaded and ready to burst.

Sighted

Against the steel-grey
thunderous
tight-as-a-drum-skin
threatening sky,
I watch a brilliant
pure white
feathered wild-goose
dazzlingly fly.

Endangered

Sharp eyes, peeping in terror through a crack,
Slow death, rolling heavily onto its back,
Lost world, vanishing without trace or track.

Last flight home to the desolate empty nest,
Sweet song robbed of its perfect pitch and zest,
Heartbeat stilled in a stolen treasure-chest.

First came the giving, now comes the taking away,
The grabbing of greed at the end of a darkening day
And if this goes then that goes then everything may.

And a world that's been finally lost is beyond recall
Like a vast egg unmendable after its fall
Or as dead, as we say, as the dodo, and shame on us all.

The Bull
(in memory of Ted Hughes)

Look where he stands
alone in the meadow
with a brow of thunder
and a ring through his nose.

Like a heavyweight boxer
he paws at the ground
and his dangerous eyes
say *Beware! Beware!*

He could send you sky-high
with a toss of his head.
His moon-slice horns
are a Viking's helmet.

But now look again
and his strength is gentle,
at rest in the cloud
of his steaming breath.

His rough tongue licks
at his grassy muzzle
and his tail frisks nimbly
this way and that.

Oh, keep this creature
far from the ring,
from the cheering crowds,
from the blood-stained sand.

May he live here in peace,
a king among cattle,
an earth-bound god
worth his weight in gold.

A Call to Arms

The 4,000-student Bolton Institute of Higher Education . . . has
come up with a cat's collar that emits an ultrasonic sound, which
scares not the cat but the birds. At night, when all decent birds
are asleep, the collar automatically switches itself off, allowing
cats to hunt mice instead.

The Independent: 1. 7. 99

We are the birds that fly by night
Beneath the stars and moon.
From crack of dawn we're out of sight
Until late afternoon.
In other words we only wake
For our nocturnal prey
But must we call it God's mistake
That we were made that way?

The decent birds, the sunshine boys,
Have got it safe and sound
And all because the world enjoys
To see them flit around
Whereas we have our work cut out
And we just don't think it's right,
So raise your beaks with us and shout
Indecent birds, unite!

Wordsworth's Watering Can

William Wordsworth named his watering can Kubla after Coleridge's 'Kubla Khan'—according to George Kirkby, a long-serving guide at Dove Cottage who has recreated the garden there.

Wordsworth loved his garden,
a small one as gardens go,
just a patch behind Dove Cottage
but beautiful, even so.

And he loved his sister, Dorothy.
They tended the flowers together.
This is the life, they thought,
Oh, why can't it last for ever!

So they drenched their dry earth daily
with Kubla whose trusty spout
recalled those measureless caverns
as it fountained the water about.

In the Book of Life it is written:
*No greater love hath man
than that he should choose his friend's poem
as the name for a watering can.*

The Last Day of the Holidays

The day that I fell and cut my chin
Was a terrible day with the tide coming in
And the sky overhead like a sheet of steel
And something wrong with my bicycle wheel
And nothing at all when I squeezed the brakes
And no one to point out my mistakes
And the rain coming down in buckets of wet
And the future as grim as the lecture I'd get
And everything wobbling out of control
And as I remember it, body and soul,
The day that I fell and cut my chin
With the rain coming down and the tide coming in
Was the day that I felt growing up begin.

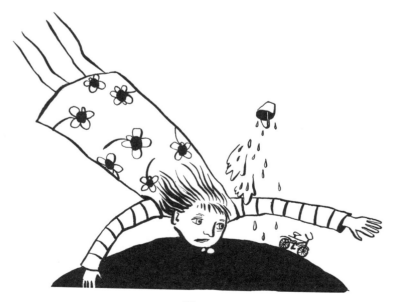

Remembrance Day Remembered

For the sake of men we never knew
We trooped into the hall
Where their names in golden letters
Were written on the wall.

Somebody sounded a bugle
And ghosts seemed everywhere
Until the last note softly fell
On the suddenly empty air.

Then the world filled up with living
In its own accustomed way,
With the usual busy traffic
Of the usual busy day.

But what I most remember
And know that I always will
Is how we stood utterly silent
And absolutely still.

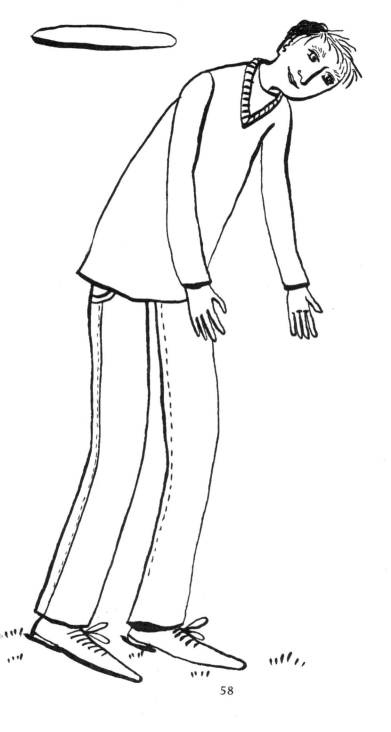

Natural Elevation

He was a tall man,
yes,
the tallest
in our world,
at least
four times as high
as Shrimp,
a human
periscope.
We asked him
'Lofty,
what's it
like
up there
and how do you
reach
your shoes
when the laces
come undone
and are there
any exercises
we could try?'

He was a quiet man, too,
but always
good at
answers
which took time
to reach us
from his altitude
as if they
came down
biblically
for our enlightenment.
'Or is it all
done with stilts?'
we giggled.
'Boys,' he replied,
'it's all to do
with life
and natural elevation
as you'll find one day
if ever you grow
half as tall
as me.'

The Philosophy of Table Manners

'Eat your greens,
don't spill the beans,
or drop a hot potato.
It's very rude
to chew your food
at more than the medium rate—O

and if you do
I'm telling you,'
said Socrates to Plato,
'you'll grow as fat
as an over-fed cat
or an Eastern potentate—O'

Wrapping Up Well

Wrapping up well is the warmth still inside you
however the world tries to take it away
and if you should look like a sack of potatoes
it's much better than freezing any day.

It's two gloved fists plunged deep in your pockets,
a scarf round your mouth and the tip of your nose
and a pair of boots which your socks may feel tight in
but with just enough room to wiggle your toes.

Wrapping up well is a serious business
which comes with a warning to take good care,
to give thanks for the luck of the warmth inside you
and to do what you can for the world elsewhere.

Thinking of You

Sometimes I think of you
the way that the thinnest
wisp of a cloud
teased out
to gauzy mist
drifts off across the blue,

but sometimes too
the dark sky loaded with thunder
presses down
like a slab of stone
which I lie under
thinking of you.

Two Face

Cross my heart
And cross my fingers,
The deed is done
But the memory lingers.

In the name of truth
I told a lie
So watch your back
When I pass by.

Friends Again?

When snow melts to slush
And noise becomes hush,
When smile answers frown
And upside turns down,
When bitter tastes sweet
And both our ends meet
Then a flash in the pan
Will be what we began.

When each finds the other
And lose is discover,
When feeble feels strong
And short stretches to long,
When head rules the heart
And we make a fresh start,
Then if No or if Yes
Will be anyone's guess.